AF658044

Bookosmia

For Kids, By kids

Story Copyright © Authors Naincy and Adhishri Aruman
Designer: Prarthana Merchant
Publisher: Bookosmia
ISBN NO- 978-93-6045-350-3

Constitution Land

THIS BOOK BELONGS TO

____

____

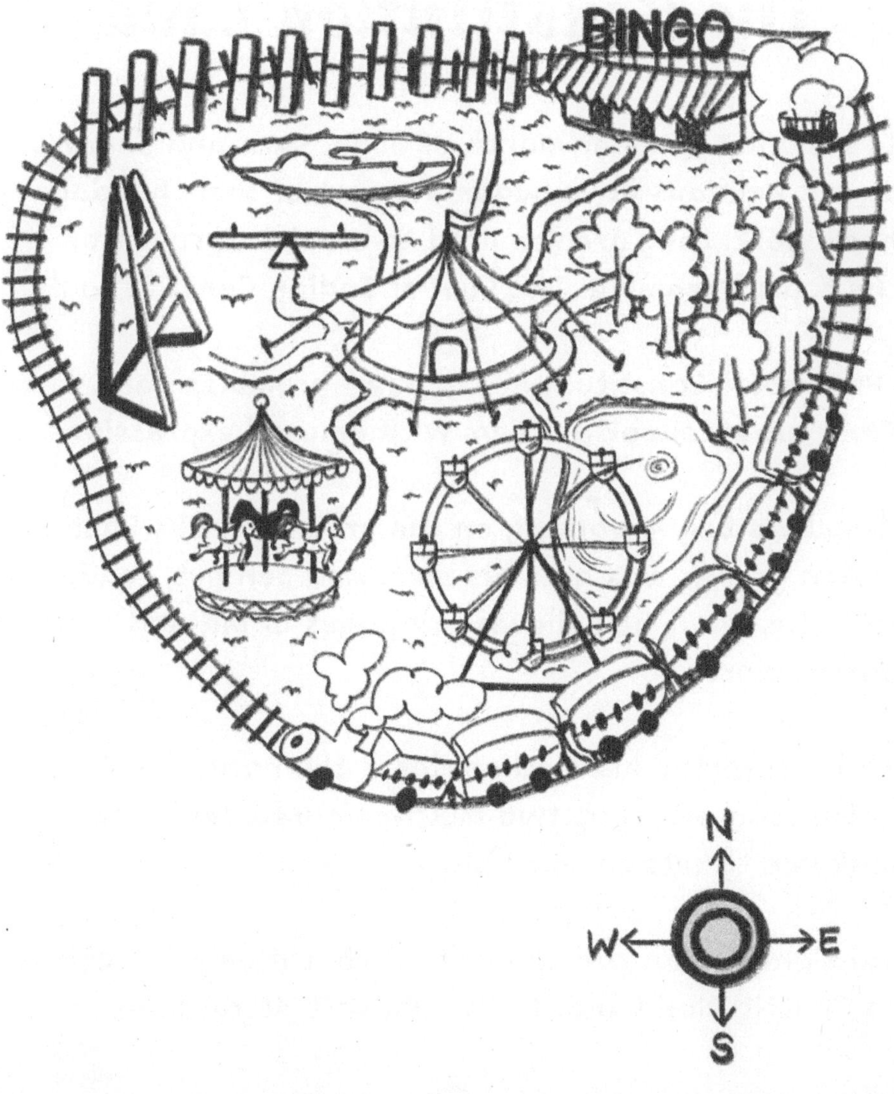
BINGO
N
W
E
S

CHAPTER 1

The Constitution Land

It's the hot summer month of June. Sara and Shaan's school holidays have begun. As part of their holiday homework, they are required to create a project on the topic 'Preamble: The Soul of Indian Constitution'.

"Preamble? Constitution? Zzzzzz," grumbles Sara. Their parents look at them with amused expressions.

"Shall we begin working on the project?" asks Papa. Shaan groans and gets his book and pen out, ready to write, what he believes are pages of big and boring words.

To his surprise, his mother closes the book. She animatedly holds up two multi-coloured sheets that look like tickets to some place.

Sara and Shaan run up to read what it says. 'Ticket to Constitution Land: India's newest attraction'

"An amusement park trip?" Sara and Shaan scream aloud. This project has started out like no other!

Today they are on a learning expedition to visit India's newest attraction, **The Constitution Land.**

QUESTION

The document of the highest law in India was hand-written by Prem Behari Narain Raizada. The original document is now kept in a helium-filled case in the library of the Indian Parliament House.
What document are we talking about?

Answer: The Indian Constitution
The only handwritten constitution in the world

At the entry of the big "Constitution Land", they are handed citizen cards, a one-time pass for all the rides. The card states:

> **"Welcome to the land of the largest written constitution of the world. We, the people of India, adopted, enacted and gave ourselves this constitution on the 26th November 1949. You, the citizen, today get the chance to explore the rights it bestows upon us and the principles of governance it sets out for us."**

Shaan is curious and asks his mother, "Mumma, who are the 'we' in **'We, the people of India'** mentioned here?"

His mother tells him, "Kanna, when India was freed of British rule after years of struggle, it was recognised as an independent republic with the citizens, laws, and government of its own. 'We' in 'We, the people of India' are those citizens of that independent union of the Indian republic and the citizens now. It's us - you, me, all of us in the country... It's 'We, the people of India'.

Sara is even more curious now and asks her father, "Papa, what is a citizen?" Her father tells her, "Beta, a citizen is a *person who is a member of a country and has the rights and protections granted by its constitution*. Citizens hold a say in how their country is governed."

QUESTION

You are in a group project at school with 8 other classmates. How does "We the People" in the Preamble relate to the idea that the power of the government ultimately comes from the citizens?

a. Convince all members about your decisions as best
b. Accept others decision without understanding to keep them happy
c. Consider the best interest of all group members
d. Fight among each other and work individually

Answer: c. Consider the best interest of all group members

"We the People" in the Preamble reminds us that the government is formed by the people and for the people. In our group project, it means that the decisions we make should consider the best interests of all group members, just like the government should consider the well-being of all citizens.

FACT

India holds the record for the largest democratic election in the world, with over 900 million eligible voters participating in the 2019 general elections.

The guide, handing out little maps to everyone announces, "Hello everyone! 'Constitution Land', as you can see, is designed on the layout of the **preamble**, often known as the ***'mini-constitution'***. The map that you hold also features the preamble, and as we go through different rides, we will be learning the meaning of the important terms of the preamble. Let's get started with 'The Sovereign Socialist Secular See-saw'!"

"Hurrah! Let's go!"

CHAPTER 2

Sovereign Socialist Secular See-saw

Welcome to the "Sovereign Socialist Secular See-saw" at Constitution Land, where you, the young citizens of this country, will make sure that our see-saw remains balanced. Imagine a giant see-saw, perfectly balanced in the middle. On one end, we have words like sovereignty, socialism, and secularism, words that we find in the preamble of our constitution. And on the other end, we will see ideas or influences that may disturb the see-saw balance. This see-saw is our symbol for the *balance* required for running a country like India.

Imagine your classroom with your classmates, the furniture, your belongings like your books, bag etc and your teacher. Now imagine that your classroom is a country, and as residents of your classroom country, you will want to make some rules for your country,

right? Like, extending your lunch time? Or maybe adding more sports time to your schedule? How would you feel if someone else, say from another school, made these decisions for you? You probably will not like it, right? When you, and by you, we mean *everyone* in your class, will take decisions for the class collectively and the decisions will not be taken by any external people, you will become a **sovereign classroom country.**

In the preamble, we the citizens of India have declared that we are a sovereign country. A country that makes its own laws. A country that is independent and not 'under' any other control. This does not mean that we will stop interacting with other countries or not do trade with them. Just like in your sovereign classroom country, you will be friends with students from other classrooms and work with them, say on projects or annual day celebrations. Sovereignty simply means that as a country, we will have all the authority and power to deal with all our issues without any external interference.

Now, going back to your classroom country, think about the situations in which your sovereignty, or your control over your classroom country, may become threatened?

DISCUSS IN CLASS AND WRITE A FEW SITUATIONS DOWN IN THE SPACE GIVEN.

In a similar way, our country's sovereignty may also face threats and dangers in the following situations:

1. Another country declaring war on us can challenge our sovereignty

2. External pressure on us to do something we don't want to do

3. Other countries or organisations interfering with our elections.

The sovereignty see-saw has the authority of the country and its people on one side and external pressure on the other. We have to keep making sure that the see-saw does not lose its balance by our actions such as:

1. Maintaining friendly and mutually beneficial relationships with other countries,

2. Practising strong and stable governance and legal mechanisms through local and central government and courts.

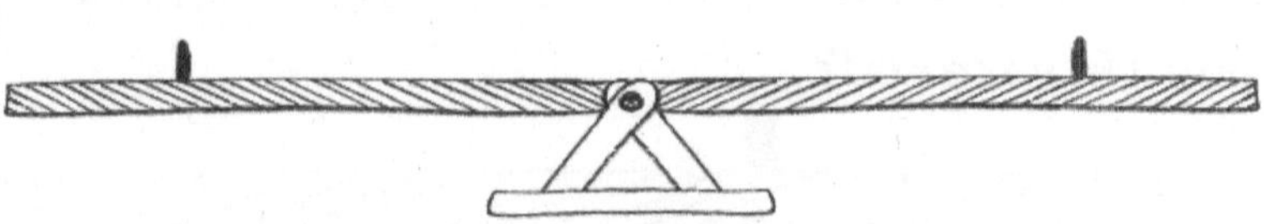

3. Making elections free and fair so that no one can question our intent and transparency

QUESTION

Your school is planning to host a special inter school event, and you have a lot of decisions to make. How can you apply/relate to the concept of "sovereignty" in such a scenario?

a. Wait for other school's advice
b. Be scared to take decisions
c. Be influenced by other people's opinion
d. Take decisions independently

Answer: d. Take decisions independently

In this scenario, "sovereignty" means that your school has the power to make its own decisions without being controlled by other schools or external forces.

FACT

India's nuclear tests in 1998 demonstrated its sovereign decision-making in matters of national security, despite international pressures.

The next terms on our see-saw are socialist and secular. Interestingly, these words were not a part of the original preamble but were added by the Indian government in 1976. Let's see what they mean for us as Indian citizens but also for our classroom country?

Let's start with **socialist**. Going back to your classroom country, you may have some things that everyone uses, for example, the board, the furniture, maybe some charts or toys and so on.

Who owns these things? No one single person like you, your friend or your teacher owns them, right? You all use them to learn and teach and in one way, you all own them. You all are trusted with the responsibility of taking good care of them, not damaging them intentionally or not taking them back home for your personal use. Everyone takes care of them and uses them for their benefit. This is the idea of socialism. That property or natural resources should not be owned by one person but by the society as a whole. For example, no one person owns the Indian Railways but we all use them. The money we pay as taxes to the government, is used to run and maintain the railways, pay the employees and enhance the railway network.

QUESTION

You and your friends cross a lane with people living in tents who do not even have basic needs like food, water and shelter fulfilled. By running a donation campaign to collect funds for their upliftment, what principle from the Indian Constitution's preamble do you exhibit?

a. Socialism
b. Sovereignty
c. Liberty
d. Fraternity

Answer: a. Socialism

"Socialism" in the Preamble means that we should work to reduce inequalities and help those in need. Collecting items for a local shelter is an act of socialism because it shows we care about the well-being of everyone in our community.

FACT

The Mahatma Gandhi National Rural Employment Guarantee Act (MGNREGA) in India is a socialist program that provides guaranteed employment to rural citizens, helping to alleviate poverty.

Secular may be a word you have heard before. In the preamble, secular means that the government is separate from any religion or religious beliefs. In one way it means that the government allows citizens to practise any religions they believe and, in another way, it means that the law will not discriminate among citizens on the basis of their religion. It also means that our country does not have an official or national religion. Will you choose an official religion for your classroom country?

DISCUSS WITH YOUR CLASSMATES.

____

____

The socialist and secular see-saw will be balanced if citizens are able to enjoy their right to practise the religion of their choice freely and if they are able to access resources and opportunities equally.

QUESTION

In your class, there are students from various religious backgrounds. Diwali vacation is approaching. How can you demonstrate "secularism" when discussing holidays or traditions?

a. While you talk about Diwali, ask your classmates from other religions to also share about their festivals

b. Argue that your religion is the best

c. Make friends with only those of your religion

d. Talk about why only religion of the majority matters

Answer: a. Ask classmates of other religions to also share

"Secularism" means respecting and treating all religions equally. When discussing holidays or traditions, you should be inclusive, acknowledging and respecting the beliefs and customs of all your classmates, not favoring one over the others.

FACT

The Ajmer Sharif Dargah and the Golden Temple in Amritsar are prominent examples of religious places in India, showcasing the nation's commitment to secularism by welcoming people of all faiths.

WHY IS BALANCE IMPORTANT?

In a playground, if a see-saw is heavily weighted on one side, it won't function properly. It's the same with a country. Balance in the constitution ensures that no single principle overpowers the others, which could lead to tyranny, inequality, or dissatisfactions among citizens. A well-balanced constitution promotes harmony, supports stability, and ensures that diverse perspectives contribute to the nation's welfare.

Trivia

The word sovereign in the Indian constitution was taken from article 5 of Ireland's constitution, which states that – The state is declared "sovereign, independent, and democratic".

CHAPTER 3

The Democratic Domino

Let's go back to your classroom country for a while. Have you thought of a name for your classroom country?

DISCUSS SOME POSSIBLE NAMES FOR THIS COUNTRY - TAKE SUGGESTIONS FROM YOUR CLASSMATES AND YOUR TEACHER. LETS SAY, THERE ARE 5 SUGGESTIONS.

____

____

How will you choose the final name? What will be the criteria for the final name? Should the name be an already existing word or a new word altogether?

One way of making these decisions could be randomly choosing the name using a coin flip or say by writing each name on pieces of paper and choosing one of them. Another way could be by taking a vote from all the classmates and going ahead with the one that gets the maximum vote. What is the difference between both the approaches?

DISCUSS

____

____

The second approach can be called a democratic approach of making a decision and **democracy** is also one of the words used in the preamble. Surely, you all have heard of this word before and know the meaning of it somewhat. When India became independent, the country decided that we will be a democratic country. That is, we will take our decisions as a collective, counting everyone's opinions. Especially, when it will be about choosing our representatives, the members of our government, we will make sure that everyone gets to have a say in choosing them. This was made possible through elections at all levels of government. *From the local to the national level, we vote in the elections and choose who we want as our leaders.*

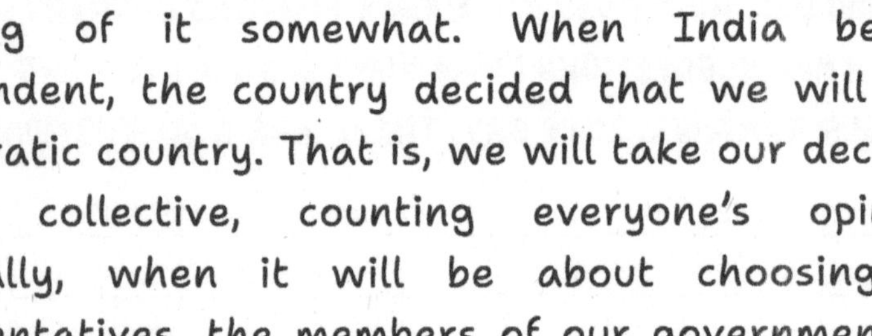

QUESTION

Your school needs to choose a grade representative, for each grade and you have multiple ways to do this. You choose to organize an election and vote for an eligible candidate. What principle of the Indian constitution's preamble relates to this process?

a. Democracy
b. Socialism
c. Secularism
d. Fraternity

Answer: a. Democracy

Using a vote to choose a grade representative is a democratic process. It ensures that everyone has a say in who gets elected, just like in a democracy where people elect their leaders through voting.

FACT

The Right to Information (RTI) Act allows Indian citizens to actively participate in the democratic process by providing them with the means to request information from government institutions, policies, and decisions promoting transparency and citizen participation

But the functioning of this democracy is completely dependent on you and me, the citizens of this country. Even if one of us does not participate in the democratic practices in our country, the democracy domino will fall. The makers of our constitution knew this, they knew that until every adult citizen had the right to vote and express their choice, irrespective of their class, caste, gender, religion, democracy will not function at its best. They made sure that the democracy domino remains intact, and that each citizen has equal rights to participate in the great democracy in India. This also refers to the political equality that all Indian citizens enjoy, you will learn more about it in the chapter on equality.

QUESTION

Mysore Paints and Varnish Limited is the only company that manufacturers a particular product in India. They export this product to 30 other countries as well.

Name this product, that is mainly required during elections.

Answer: Indelible Ink - Ink that cannot be erased or washed away.

It is applied to the forefinger (usually) of voters during elections in order to prevent electoral fraud such as double voting.

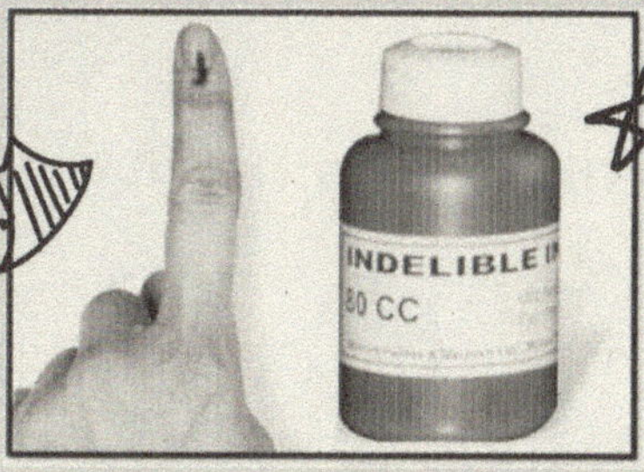

Think about how you will ensure that the democracy domino of your classroom country will remain intact?

Now go back to your classroom country for a while. Have you finalized a name for your classroom country? How did you go about it? Did you ask for everyone in class to vote for the shortlist? Did the teacher or class monitors vote matter more?

WRITE ABOUT YOUR APPROACH.

____

____

QUESTION

A country that borders India on the North was until recently, a monarchy. A prolonged people's movement succeeded in ending the monarchy's power and establishing democracy in 2006. The people of this country adopted a new Constitution in 2015.

Name the country that meets the above description.

Answer: Nepal.

Monarchy is a form of government that often involves a single, hereditary ruler who holds significant power and authority over the state.

CHAPTER 4

The Republic Railway

Let's now board the Republic Railway, a grand train ride through Constitution Land! This railway represents the Republic of India, a *state in which supreme power is held by the people and their elected representatives.* This means that as a country, we have an elected or nominated president rather than a monarch. The train itself symbolises the journey of the Indian Republic—a journey toward democracy, justice, and equality. Each station along the way marks a significant milestone in the establishment and evolution of the Republic, reflecting how the constitution supports and enhances the lives of its citizens.

Just as a railway connects distant places and people, making travel possible across regions, the concept of a republic connects the people of India to their government. It ensures that all citizens, irrespective of their identity and background, have a voice in how the country is run.

In this journey through the Republic, let us see how the train looks like.

Trivia

Milestones of the Republic

The Formation of the Republic: India became a republic on January 26, 1950. This date marked the full transition from a dominion with the British monarch as head of state to a fully sovereign state with a constitutionally elected leader, celebrating the birth of the Indian Republic.

THE ENGINE: SOVEREIGNTY

The engine of the Republic Railway is *mighty and self-driven*, symbolising India's sovereignty. Opposite to it are heavy chains representing colonial rule. As we discussed earlier, sovereignty means India as a country drives itself without any external controls, free from colonial constraints. The engine must be powerful enough to pull the entire train, ensuring that the chains of external control do not drag it back. *Sovereignty propels the train forward, illustrating self-governance and independence.*

In other words, *sovereignty implies that India is its own boss, free from external control or influence.* It's like having a remote control that only India holds, which directs how the country runs, makes laws, and interacts with other nations. While, *republic refers to a state where the public (the people of India) has the ultimate power through their right to vote.* They elect representatives, including the President, who acts not as a monarch but as a servant of the people's will. This is like passengers on a train electing their conductor who ensures the journey respects the route chosen by the passengers themselves.

THE PASSENGER CARS: FEDERALISM

Multiple cars connected flexibly yet firmly, each car representing a state or a union territory, showcasing India's federal structure. *Federalism in India signifies that while there is a central government, each state has its own government which governs alongside the central authority.* Each car must align well with the others, ensuring the train runs smoothly. *Effective communication and cooperation between the central and state governments ensure that the passenger cars (states) remain well-connected, and the journey (governance) is harmonious.* We will learn more about Fraternity in an upcoming chapter.

THE CABOOSE: SECULARISM

The caboose, or the last car, acts as a safeguard, ensuring that no religious bias creeps into the governance as the train moves forward. Secularism ensures that the state keeps an equal distance from all religions, promoting a fair governance system where religion does not influence legal and state matters. It stabilizes the train by being a neutral, balancing force, ensuring that the journey does not tilt towards any religious bias. If the caboose sways towards any religious majority, it could derail the train, causing instability in the secular fabric of the nation.

QUESTION

The Constitution gave the citizens of India the power to choose their own government and paved the way for democracy.

A national holiday is celebrated annually to commemorate the adoption of the constitution of India on January 26, 1950. It differs from Independence Day, which annually commemorates the end of British rule on August 15, 1947.

What day is it?

Answer: Republic day

India is a republic, which means our country doesn't have a king or queen. Instead, we elect our leaders, like the President, through a fair and open process.

FACT

Dr. Rajendra Prasad was the first President of the Republic of India when the nation adopted its Constitution on January 26, 1950.

CHAPTER 5

The Liberty Ladder

Freedom. A term that you must have heard very often. The freedom struggle. Indian independence.

Liberty is just another word for freedom, a synonym. Liberty is the root on which the seed of justice rests and grows. Liberty means that all the citizens of our country are free to do whatever they choose to do, practise any religion and mannerisms freely, and go wherever they'd like just as freely. However, this freedom is not absolute. This means that citizens are free to do whatever they want until it causes harm or threat to another citizen or is in opposition to the rule of law established by our constitution.

QUESTION

There are individual liberties and protections guaranteed by a constitution. They include the right to equality, freedom of speech, and the right to life and personal liberty. They form a cornerstone of the Indian Constitution.

What are they collectively called?

Answer: Fundamental Rights

Right to freedom is also one of the six fundamental rights of our constitution. In order to reach the 'Justice Jigsaw', you are required to climb this two-step liberty ladder. Every step provides you, the young citizen, with different kinds of liberties, which make an Indian citizen a free citizen.

The first step of the ladder provides the citizens with **social liberties**. These include freedom to choose the ways one would like to live their lives, which include freedom to practise any religion, freedom of movement, to move or reside freely in any part of the country, freedom to dress as one would want and the freedom to follow one's own unique cultural practices.

The second step of the ladder provides citizens with **political liberties**. These include freedom of speech, expression and thought. This freedom comes with a reasonable restriction, like any other freedom. This means that all the citizens are free to express their beliefs and voice out their opinions till the time it is against the national interests or defames another citizen.

Congratulations, you have climbed the liberty ladder! You are now free and ready to enter a just society.

QUESTION

You and your classmates are being given a reading challenge where each of you has to read 30 books. How can your teacher apply the principle of "liberty" in such a task?

a. Force students to read the books your teacher selects
b. Make sure you choose the book that your friend chooses
c. Not give access to the books of your choice
d. Give you the freedom to choose books of your choice

Answer:
d. Give you the freedom to choose books of your choice

Allowing students to choose their own books for reading assignments is an example of "liberty." It means you have the freedom to make choices that suit your interests and preferences.

Trivia

Our constitution grants us six fundamental rights. They are "fundamental" because they are considered essential for a harmonious and peaceful society and for ensuring the quality of life of our citizens. Other than the right to freedom, the other five fundamental rights are:

- ✓ Right to equality
- ✓ Right against exploitation
- ✓ Right to constitutional remedies
- ✓ Cultural and Educational rights
- ✓ Right to freedom of religion

Trivia

None of the rights granted to the citizens are absolute, and there is a reasonable restriction that can be imposed on these rights. A reasonable restriction ensures that the citizens are able to enjoy their rights without causing a nuisance to anyone, and is usually imposed by the state.

CHAPTER 6

The Justice Jigsaw

Justice stands for a single rule of law for all, an equal grant of rights, an equal offer of opportunities, and an equal voice in all decisions of a country. Justice is an ideal that we are always working towards, and a fundamental principle enlisted in the preamble of our constitution.

Welcome to 'The Justice Jigsaw'. You, the young citizen, are now required to find the pieces of social, economic and political justice and solve this jigsaw in order to ensure equality in the country, and move to the Equality Bingo.

Let's go back to our classroom country. The school rules, the uniform etiquettes, the books, the tables and chairs you sit on, all remain the same and equal for all, right? The teacher teaches everyone the same thing in the class. No one is treated differently because they look a certain way, are a boy or girl, practise a certain religion, or are born in a particular city. This is what the idea of **social justice** represents. And that's your first piece of the jigsaw.

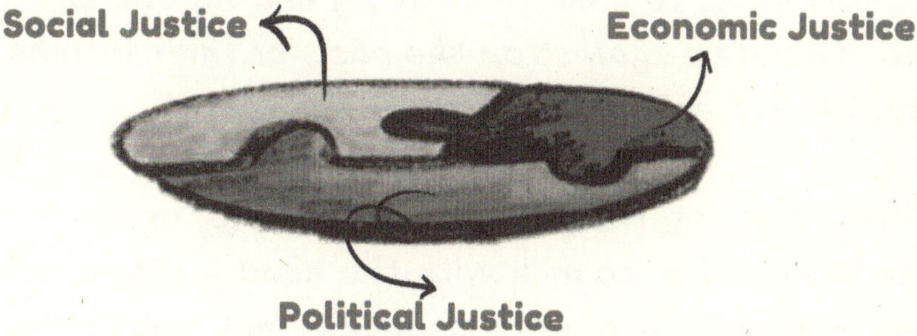

SOCIAL JUSTICE:

No citizen is discriminated against on the basis of caste, creed, colour, religion, gender or place of birth. This means that the rule of law set out by our constitution remains the same for all the citizens regardless of their social positioning in the society.

Does every child you know go to a school like yours or they go different types of schools? And do you have the same access to all the school facilities as your other classmates? Are you offered and encouraged for the same opportunities as your classmates? If yes, then that's economic justice, your second piece of the puzzle.

ECONOMIC JUSTICE:

All citizens are provided with the same economic opportunities to earn their living and no one is discriminated against on the basis of their income, wealth and economic status.

While choosing the monitor of the class, or electing the prefectorial council with the head girl and head boy, you are given a fair chance to not just stand for the elections, voice your opinions, but also choose who will represent you. This is what the third and the last piece of our 'Justice Jigsaw', political justice, stands for.

POLITICAL JUSTICE:

All citizens have equal political rights and opportunities to participate in the political processes and decisions of our country. The adoption of Universal Adult Franchise ensures that this ideal is achieved. Universal Adult Franchise states that all citizens who are 18 years and above are free to vote and their vote has an equal value regardless of their caste or education, religion, colour, race, and economic conditions.

That completes your 'Justice Jigsaw'. You can now enjoy your next equal activity, 'The Equality Bingo'.

QUESTION

You and your friends are playing an interesting game. Your friend is (perhaps wrongly) accused of cheating in the game.

How can you support "justice" in this situation?

a. Punish your friend
b. Give your friend a chance to explain
c. Never play with your friend again
d. Tease your friend in front of others

Answer: b. Give your friend a chance to explain

Supporting "justice" in this situation means ensuring your friend gets a fair chance to explain themselves and isn't unfairly punished. You can help by being fair and listening to all sides of the story.

FACT

The Supreme Court of India played a pivotal role in ensuring justice during the famous Kesavananda Bharati case,(also known as the Fundamental Rights Case) which affirmed the supremacy of the Indian Constitution. Find out more about it.

CHAPTER 7

The Equality Bingo

The constitution of India aims to achieve the goal of equality. All other principles are in the pursuance of equality. *Equality is a state in which all citizens hold equal status (economic, social and political) in the society and are provided with just as equal opportunities for growth and development.* The preamble of our constitution not just states the **equality of status and opportunity**, it directs the state to work for the **promotion of such equality.**

"Equality Bingo"

This is the 'Equality Bingo'. Everyone will be handed a card with various scenarios on it. Scenarios will be announced and you have to decide if that is a scenario in which everyone is equal. Everyone will have an equal opportunity to cancel out the unequal scenarios as they are announced.

Scenario 1: Your classmate skipped a test because they were sick. The teacher decided to take a retest.

Scenario 2: You have to give the same level of maths as your seniors.

Scenario 3: During the annual day selections, everyone is given an equal opportunity to participate in the events.

The first scenario here may seem unequal, but actually depicts what is called equity. *Equity is exercised to ensure that each person with different circumstances is treated in manners and provided differential opportunities needed to reach an equal outcome.* Because your classmate was sick, they could not prepare or sit for the exam. In order to ensure equality, the teacher gives them another opportunity as a retest.

The second scenario is visibly unequal. You cannot be expected to give the same level of maths test as your seniors, because your level of knowledge and their level of knowledge is not equal. Hence, this should be cancelled out.

The third scenario clearly depicts equality, as you are given a fair chance to participate in the annual day. Bingo! You nailed it!

QUESTION

Your school is conducting the yearly sports day event, and you have been given the responsibility of organizing events. How can you ensure that everyone has an equal opportunity to participate, regardless of their abilities?

a. Organise different categories and events
b. Choose your friend's favourite sport for the competition
c. Discourage students who are not interested in sports
d. Give more chance for students of a particular religion

Answer: a. Organise different categories and events

To ensure "equality" in sports day, you can organize different categories or events where students of various abilities can participate and have a chance to win. This promotes fairness and equal opportunities for all.

FACT

India has made strides toward gender equality with women holding important positions in government, such as Indira Gandhi, who served as India's first female Prime Minister.

CHAPTER 8

The Fraternity Fun Zone

Now onto the Fraternity Fun Zone, a lively and inclusive park in Constitution Land where the *spirit of sisterhood, brotherhood and community thrives.* Here, every ride, game, and attraction are designed to foster *unity and mutual respect* among India's diverse population. The fun zone is a place where children and adults from various backgrounds come together, celebrating the richness and the diversity of Indian culture.

Fraternity, or brotherly/ sisterly love, is essential in a diverse country like India because it binds different cultures, languages, and religions together in a shared sense of nationhood. Imagine your classroom country and how you may be. Just as a fun zone is more joyful when everyone plays together harmoniously, a nation thrives when its people work together towards common goals, respecting and valuing each other's differences.

QUESTION

Your class decides to organize a cleanup drive in the neighborhood park.

How can you demonstrate "fraternity" in this community service project?

a. Show your power and dominate in the drive
b. Working together with your classmates and the community
c. Work only with your friends
d. Displaying gender discrimination

Answer: b. Working together with your classmates and the community

"Fraternity" means treating others like brothers and sisters, so in a cleanup drive, you can show fraternity by working together with your classmates and the community, helping each other, and creating a sense of unity and togetherness.

FACT

The Indian Railways, one of the world's largest railway networks, promotes fraternity by connecting people from diverse backgrounds and regions, fostering unity and cooperation.

THE MERRY-GO-ROUND: UNITY IN DIVERSITY

Imagine a grand merry-go-round with horses, chariots, and carriages representing various Indian states and ethnic groups, all moving in harmony. This ride symbolises the unity of India's diverse cultures, spinning together in joyous equilibrium. Each figure on the merry-go-round, distinct yet integral, contributes to the ride's overall motion and beauty, just like each community enriches Indian democracy. If one figure tries to move against the rhythm or overpower others, the ride becomes unstable. Maintaining equal speed and space for all ensures smooth rotation and collective enjoyment.

THE HARMONY HALL: CELEBRATING CULTURAL FESTIVALS

We also have a large hall where festivals from Diwali to Eid and Christmas are celebrated under one roof. Each festival booth is decorated to reflect its unique traditions and foods. The Harmony Hall promotes *understanding and appreciation for all religious and cultural festivities, teaching inclusiveness.* Participants share their traditions and partake in others', creating a mosaic of cultural exchange.

Exlclusion of any group can ead to a feeling of isolation and conflict. *Inclusive celebration keeps the social fabric woven tightly.*

THE BRIDGE OF BELIEFS: CONNECTING HEARTS

Visualise a sturdy bridge with various religious and cultural symbols engraved on its rails, crossing a scenic river. This bridge represents the connection between different beliefs, facilitating a respectful passage from one understanding to another. As people cross the bridge, they experience views from all sides, symbolising perspective-taking and empathy. A bridge without strong support (mutual respect and understanding) can collapse. Ensuring that the bridge is well-maintained with the pillars of respect ensures safe and enriching crossings for everyone.

QUESTION

This is a Propaganda Poster from 1793 representing the French First Republic with the Slogan: "Unity and Indivisibility of the Republic: ___, ___ & ___."

What three words, originating in the French Revolution, served as the inspiration for inserting certain phrases in the Preamble of the Indian Constitution?

Answer:

"Liberté, égalité, fraternité"

"Liberty, Equality and Fraternity"

CHAPTER 9

The Assembly Treehouse

Imagine your school assembly. Students of different classes and sections standing in their designated lines. Principal's address. Class monitors representing each class. Students of different houses. Red. Green. Blue. Yellow. But all in one uniform. All belonging to the same class. All in the same assembly.

Welcome to 'The Assembly Treehouse'. This treehouse features the various committees and their representatives of the constituent assembly. Just like your school assembly, the constituent assembly was made of representatives from different parts of our country who sat together for 2 years, 11 months and 18 days to draft the largest constitution of the world, the Indian Constitution. This assembly represented and voiced the ideas, demands and views of our very culturally diverse country. And just like your school principal, the constituent assembly was presided by

Dr. Rajendra Prasad.

The chairman of the drafting committee, **Dr. B. R. Ambedkar**, also famously known as the father of the Indian constitution for his remarkable contributions towards the *ideals of equality and justice* is also housed in this treehouse.

This brings us to the end of 'The Constitution Land'. The exit is that way. We hope you have learnt a little more about our constitution and the ideals it promotes and are leaving as a more informed citizen. If you forget anything, you can always refer to the preamble, which truly harbours the *soul of our constitution.*

Reviews

"This book opens like a treasure hunt and an invitation to discover the world of our foundational values - the Constitution of India. Bringing it alive through engaging bite sized facts and unbundles complex concepts of the essence of the Constitution in a fun way. The thoughtful design makes it feel like a personal diary - my interactive personal Constitution. I had fun with it and I am sure it will bring meaningful engaging moments on an important conversation for parents and children alike"

- Deepika Mogilishetty, Chief of Policy & Partnerships - EkStep Foundation

"We are a diverse country, with hundreds of languages and cultures, some followed by a few thousands, and others by millions. It is the Constitution that can ensure we all have equal rights under the law. It is critical that young Indians see the principles outlined in our Constitution as not mere words but living, breathing workable ideals of equality and justice. This book is an attempt to do that."

- Priti David, Executive Editor of the People's Archive of Rural India (PARI)

"This book is an attempt to share knowledge of our constitution with children and preserve our constitution through them."

- Tushar and Chirajeet, IIM alumni and initial sponsors

CMCA congratulates Bookomania for developing 'Constitutional Land'! The book beautifully brings the Preamble of our Constitution closer to children. We look forward to using this valuable resource in our own Constitutional values programs and in our efforts to transform the young into concerned, thinking and active citizens.

- Priya Krishnamurty, CEO and Co-founder, CMCA

Do you know Bookosmia publishes thoughts and ideas of students like you from 150+ locations?

Share some/all of the answers to the prompts in this book with sara@bookosmia.com and get digitally published too.

Bookosmia

For Kids, By kids

Created by

Naincy is a sociologist and works at Ashoka University. She is a co-founder of Project Cornelia, an NGO committed to work constitutional & democratic literacy among young citizens & women.

Adhishri Aruman is a graduate in Social and Public Policy from The London School of Economics and Political Science and Research Expert at Project Cornelia.

Prarthana Merchant, a visual designer, is grateful for her journey from Srishti Institute, Bangalore to a scholarship at UAL, London, for her Master's. She is passionate about storytelling to foster positive change.